FARM DOGS

A Celebration of the Farm's Hardest Worker

Text by CAROL DAVIS
Photography by NORVIA BEHLING

Voyageur Press

First published in 2007 by Voyageur Press, an imprint of MBI Publishing Company, Galtier Plaza, Suite 200, 380 Jackson Street, St. Paul, MN 55101 USA

MBI Publishing Company titles are also available at discounts in bulk quantity for industrial or sales-promotional use. For details write to Special Sales Manager at MBI Publishing Company, Galtier Plaza, Suite 200, 380 Jackson Street, St. Paul, MN 55101 USA.

To find out more about our books, join us online at www.voyageurpress.com.

On the cover: Border collies are wonderful herders. Their instinct and boundless energy combine to form a great sheep dog.

On the frontispiece: A farm dog's instinct is intact from the time he or she is a puppy and will continue to develop as the pup grows.

On the title pages: Farm dogs are known for their intelligence, keen eye, protectiveness, loyalty, unwavering work ethic, and status as good all-around companions.

On the back cover: *(top left)* At the end of a long day, the farm dog will be there to escort you back to the house, collapse on the porch, and be ready and waiting to do it all over again the next day. *(bottom left)* No matter where the farm truck goes, the farm dog is always ready to hop in and go for a ride. *(bottom right)* Border collies have a lot of instinctual talents for herding, but to have your dog be the best herder, formal training is recommended.

ISBN-13: 978-0-7603-2801-9
ISBN-10: 0-7603-2801-3

Library of Congress Cataloging-in-Publication Data

Davis, Carol, 1959-
  Farm dogs : a celebration of the farm's hardest worker
/ Carol Davis ;
photography by Norvia Behling.
      p. cm.
  Includes index.
  ISBN-13: 978-0-7603-2801-9 (plc w/ jacket)
  ISBN-10: 0-7603-2801-3 (plc w/ jacket)
  1. Working dogs. 2. Livestock protection dogs.
  3. Herding dogs. 4.
Cattle dogs. 5. Sheep dogs. 6. Border collie. I. Behling,
Norvia.
II. Title.
SF428.6.D38 2007
636.73--dc22
                                        2006039124

Editor: Amy Glaser
Designer: Brenda C. Canales

Printed in China

Most farm dogs begin their lives around livestock.

Chapter 1

FARM AND RANCH DOGS

BRED TO BE VALUABLE PARTNERS

ONE DAY IN 1972, an agricultural official with the University of California visited Catherine de la Cruz's dairy farm in Sonoma and asked her to fill out some forms outlining the livestock she had lost to predators.

"I said, 'We don't have any,' and he said, 'You *have* to have them. Everybody is having losses to coyotes.' But we didn't have any predator loss," she says. That's because de la Cruz had guardian livestock dogs that stayed with her livestock to fend off coyotes, dogs, and other predators. The idea of livestock guardians was a novel one in the United States at the time, but the next decades saw farmers and ranchers turning to them to successfully cut their losses.

Visit a farm—any kind, any size—and you'll without a doubt encounter a farm dog. It may be a Great Pyrenees, as

Young dogs who are born and raised around livestock grow up to have no fear around them.

de la Cruz had, a Border collie (the king of the herding dogs), a kelpie, terrier, heeler, or a dog of mixed origin, whose diluted bloodlines contain a little of this and a little of that.

Farm dogs have different duties, depending on what they're best capable of and what their bloodlines dictate. They may be herding dogs, guard dogs, children's protectors, livestock guardian dogs, family companions, or a little bit of each. More than likely, they take their responsibilities seriously and do their job very well.

There's a reason for that, and there's a captivating history for every kind of farm dog that explains why it does its particular duties so well. Today's farmers and ranchers are able to reap the benefit of hundreds, or even thousands, of years of breeding. That's why a Border collie must gather and herd

livestock: it's so inbred into their DNA that the dog doesn't have any choice. That's also why a Great Pyrenees guards its territory and everything in it with single-mindedness. That's why a cattle dog will work itself literally to death. Every dog is different, but look at the background of a handful of traditional farm dogs and you can easily see why, no matter their breed, farm dogs are such valuable partners on the farm or ranch.

This litter of puppies is cute and cuddly now, but, trained correctly, these dogs will grow up to become valuable, hard-working stock dogs.

CATAHOULA LEOPARD DOG

The Catahoula leopard dog, known as the largest and most aggressive of the cattle dogs, is believed to date back more than 400 years to Spanish explorer Hernando de Soto's time in Louisiana. The Spaniards had "war dogs," most likely the mastiff and greyhound, who guarded the camps and hunted. Dogs who were left behind by de Soto most likely bred with the red wolf, which is native to that area, and became companions to Native Americans.

About a century later, the Frenchmen who were exploring the mouth of the Mississippi River became intrigued with these light-eyed canines, according to the American Catahoula Association.

Visit just about any farm or ranch and you'll find dogs of all ages.

The French explorers discovered that the wolflike dogs could hunt game and retrieve cattle in swampy, marshy areas because of their webbed feet and keen sense of smell.

The French had brought their own dogs, including the Beauceron, which were exceptional at hunting wild boar. The explorers attempted to develop an even better hunter, protector, companion, and herder by crossing the Beauceron with these wolflike dogs, the association says. The result was the Catahoula leopard dog, so named because its point of origin is believed to be the Catahoula area of Louisiana.

Natural curiosity makes for a good, alert farm dog.

This hard-working, versatile dog is bred to find livestock in swamps, thickets, canyons, forests, mountains, and other rough, remote areas. They gather cattle and keep them bunched together so the drover can move the herd. They also circle the herd as it moves to prevent a cow from breaking away.

The Catahoula leopard, an agile, athletic dog, is territorial and protective of what is his. They're extremely intelligent, but also more psychologically primitive than most herding breeds and need consistency in training. Besides herding cattle, Catahoulas are used to hunt wild boar, raccoons, squirrels, bears, and any other prey they're introduced to.

After all the herding and guarding is done, it's time for a little rest and relaxation.

AUSTRALIAN SHEPHERD

The Australian shepherd, or Aussie as it is nicknamed, is an extremely intelligent, medium-sized dog with strong herding and guardian instincts. He's also people-oriented, eager to please, and makes a wonderful family dog.

Contrary to its name, the modern Australian shepherd is the only livestock-working breed developed in the United States. The Australian shepherd's early ancestors can be traced to New Zealand, England, Australia, and the Basque region between Spain and France. The hard-working Australian shepherd may have been so named because of its connection with Basque shepherds who migrated to the United States in the nineteenth century.

The Australian shepherd's popularity rose rapidly with the boom in Western-style horse riding after World War II, according to the American Kennel Club. The general public became familiar with the breed through appearances in movies, rodeos, horse shows, and television programs. Ranchers and

*Some farm dogs become
as protective of their
people as they are
their livestock.*

Most farm dogs, with their high intelligence, also make excellent companions for children.

farmers appreciated the dog's adaptability, intelligence, and stamina, and continued to develop the breed and strengthen its best characteristics.

Perhaps the breed's best trait is its versatility. The good-natured Aussies are used as seeing-eye dogs, as utility dogs to the physically disabled and hearing-impaired, in search-and-rescue operations, and in children's homes and nursing homes for therapy work. These dogs are happiest when they're given a job to do, be it shepherding the children, protecting the house, herding livestock, or competing in dog events.

MCNAB

A Scottish immigrant who turned to his native country for breeding stock developed the McNab dog, which, after about 100 years, is becoming more popular with American livestock ranchers. Alexander McNab emigrated to Northern California from Glasgow, Scotland, in 1868. He brought along one dog, a Scotch collie, but it soon died. In 1885, with a desire to work with the Scotch collie breed, he returned to Scotland and chose two Scotch collies, Peter and Fred. They were bred to choice shepherd females of Spanish origin that were brought to America by Basque sheepherders. The resulting offspring were called McNab shepherds, a cross that Alexander McNab perfected to head or heel livestock.

The shorthaired, medium-sized (40 to 50 pounds) McNab is agile, fast, and light on his feet. Perhaps one of the breed's most prominent features is its ears, which generally are long, pointed, and stand erect. Occasionally, one may flop over, similar to a Border collie.

The McNab is an avid hunter of deer, rabbit, and squirrels. As a stock dog, he's known to be more direct and forceful than the Border collie, not as strong-willed as the Australian cattle dog, and not as high-strung as the Kelpie. Like other herding dogs, he is intelligent, easy to teach, and loyal to—and extraordinarily protective of—his human companion.

The McNab shepherd was kept primarily on the McNab ranch for generations and isn't as widespread as

continued on page 18

Above: *For every kind of farm dog, there's a captivating history that explains why he does his particular duties so well.*

Left: *Farm dogs not only make good working dogs, but they're good company at chore time.*

15

Above: *Dogs like to tag along when it's time to take a ride.*

Right: *Australian shepherds are very versatile and happiest when they are at work*

Left: *Catahoula leopard dogs are very territorial and protective of what is "his."*

Below: *It's a dirty job, but someone has to do it, and farm dogs won't shrink from their duties.*

continued from page 15

The modern Australian shepherd, contrary to its name, is the only livestock-working breed developed in the United States.

other breeds because it initially was used only on the McNab ranch. Pups were later sold to nearby ranchers who clamored for the quality bloodline. Because the McNab was developed for function rather than looks, it didn't receive much attention beyond the Northern California region.

ANATOLIAN SHEPHERD

There's a story about the Anatolian shepherd, a guardian dog that originated in Turkey 6,000 years ago, that readily illustrates this amazing breed. From Anatolian Shepherd Dogs Worldwide:

"Many Anatolian owners have heard, and believe, the account of a Turkish shepherd and his two Anatolians who took their sheep into the mountains for summer grazing. The shepherd did not return in the fall so his fellow villagers began searching for him. They found him dead. Nearby, his flock grazed peacefully. His two Anatolians were feeding and training their litter of puppies and they were still guarding the flock."

Ancient Anatolians guarded their livestock in some of Turkey's most remote areas. A tireless worker of formidable presence, the Anatolian continues to serve as the Turkish shepherd's frontline

Left: *Today's farmers and ranchers have such quality dogs because they are able to reap the benefit of hundreds, or even thousands, of years of breeding.*

Below: *Shepherds are happiest when they're given a job to do, whether it's shepherding children, protecting the house, herding livestock, or competing in dog events.*

defense from predators, according to the American Kennel Club. The modern Anatolian has remained relatively unchanged from its ancestors because of the nature of its isolated existence. Those remote areas, combined with some of Turkey's harshest climates, require the Anatolian to make independent, intelligent decisions. For example, the dog will try to avert predators before resorting to the use of force. They will usually bark first to warn intruders off and attract their human's attention to something unusual happening. If the threat continues, their barking and behavior will escalate.

The intimidating Anatolian is large, fast, and agile, so it will frighten away predators, yet is calming and gentle with young stock. The average weight of adult dogs is 130 to 150 pounds. It's dependable about staying on the job and with its flock, as the above story illustrates. In America, where Anatolians are still considered a rare breed, they are used as guardians for an array of livestock besides sheep and goats. They'll also protect cattle, horses, llamas, poultry, and ostriches.

The key to training a stock dog is to allow it to work its way.

Chapter 2

GOOD TRAINING

THE KEY TO FARM DOGS REACHING THEIR FULL POTENTIAL

The way acclaimed livestock handler Bud Williams sees it, a well-bred stock dog knows more about working livestock than he will ever know: "So why should I suppose it would be better for me to see what needs to be done, convey my command to the dog, then have him do it, rather than let the dog learn to work the stock on his own and not have to go through a middle man?"

Williams acknowledges that his methods aren't mainstream, but he'll tell you that he's never once had a bad stock dog. "I have such a different philosophy than anyone else and it's hard for people to understand," says Williams, a Texas stock handler of more than 50 years. "Every dog has a style of work that works for them, if they're allowed to use it."

Williams' style may be all his own, but stock dog trainers generally agree that a dog's inbred, natural instinct, combined with good direction, can produce an outstanding farm dog. "I don't claim to be

a dog trainer, but I've worked with hundreds of dogs through years and what I find is, if you don't [try to] get a dog to stop what he's been bred to do for all those years and [instead] use that to help you, then you end up with a pretty good dog," Williams says.

Williams starts pups with a single command—"hey"—and the first lesson is to bring the stock to him. If the pup can't see him, then it should keep the stock going in the direction of where he last saw Williams.

Williams' training technique really isn't a technique at all. Rather, he uses methods to keep a dog's attention on the livestock, not on the handler, he wrote in an article titled "Introduction to my Stock Dog Methods" for *Ranch Dog Trainer*. "It is important that you let the pup think things out," Williams writes. "If you are throwing commands at him all the time, he can't concentrate on what he is doing."

Initially, Williams teaches a pup to stay on the opposite side of the stock from him and he usually accomplishes this by moving around himself until he determines that the pup feels comfortable. Then, he can position the dog wherever he wants by moving to the opposite position. If the stock dog comes around the herd to where he can see Williams, he will take a step toward him and say, "Get back."

"I always teach the action first, then put a command to it, not the other way around," he explains in the article. "This way I am never distracting the pup's attention from the stock, and learning is always a positive experience. He is never being scolded for doing something wrong; he is only encouraged to do things right."

The key to training a stock dog is to allow it to work its way. "A dog's basic instinct is really to go and stop animals and herd them up. They're going to naturally do that unless we work with them to do the things we want them to do," Williams says. "If a good dog is allowed to work, it knows what to do. Our instincts are usually wrong and we stop it from doing the right thing."

Of the hundreds of dogs he's worked with, Williams is hard-pressed to choose a best. "I've never had a dog that wasn't outstanding," he says. "If I take a young dog out for first time, then he's the best dog I ever had. I believe in that dog and I believe it will always do the right thing. If it doesn't, I figure it's my fault."

Some trainers start young stock dogs by putting them in a small pen with three sheep that are familiar with inexperienced dogs.

Most trainers start instructing their dogs at 8 or 10 months to a year, but others start as soon as they indicate they're ready.

Stock dogs' instincts and ability might be considered amazing, but to the dogs, well, it's all in a day's work. "The dogs I've worked with have done so many remarkable things, but to them, they weren't remarkable," Williams says.

"It was nothing for me to take two or three dogs and take 500 head of cattle in northern California with one in back, one with me, and one on the weak side, which is where cattle would most likely get away," Williams says. "I might not see the dog in back for two or three hours at a time and only occasionally see the dog on the weak side. But I didn't have to say anything to them. They knew their job and they did it well. We got to where we were going and every animal would be there."

continued on page 29

A dog's basic instinct is to move and stop animals and herd them up.

It's important to let young stock dogs think things out. If you constantly throw commands at him, he can't concentrate on what he's doing.

The biggest key is reading each dog and dealing with them individually to determine what it can and can't handle.

Above: *The dog's instinct is that they're a predator and the sheep are prey. The dog does not let prey get away and will go around to the head and stop it.*

Left: *As trainers continue instructing their dog, they modify the dog's prey drive to suit their purposes.*

Above: *If a good stock dog is allowed to work, it knows what to do.*

Right: *"I'm looking for sustained interest; something in that dog's DNA that he doesn't understand but makes him want to go to the sheep," says trainer Anna Guthrie.*

continued from page 24

Anna Guthrie, a California dog trainer, starts her young Border collies with an instinct test where she puts the pup in a small pen with three sheep familiar with inexperienced dogs. "I'm looking for sustained interest; something in that dog's DNA that he doesn't understand, but makes him want to go to the sheep," she says. "What makes them work is the instinct that they're predators and the sheep are prey. The dog does not let prey get away and it will go around to the head and stop them. As we continue training, we modify that prey drive to suit our purposes," she says.

Once they're ready, Guthrie will graduate the dogs to cattle. "It needs to have a sense of self in relation to the livestock. The whole thing works on a prey drive, but a thirty-pound dog really can't physically overtake a cow," she says. "What it really boils down to is a big game of chicken—who will have the bravery or heart to stand there and not back down."

Initially working with sheep gets her dogs ready to work cows, Guthrie says. "If they start on something that won't hurt or intimidate them in the beginning, they get more self-confidence," she says. "It's important when a dog is young to not let it get bullied or traumatized by stock. But then again, you never know whether you have a good cow dog until they get kicked. Cows kick and some dogs, the first time they encounter a kick, will just go away. Other dogs keep going and others get angry. If a dog gets angry or just blows it off, all in the line of work, you know you've got a cow-working dog."

A dog's inbred, natural instinct, combined with good direction, can produce an outstanding farm dog.

Guthrie, unlike most of her counterparts, believes in starting training at a much younger age. "Most people say to start them at 8 or 10 months to a year, but I start my dogs as soon as they tell me they're ready," she says. She introduces them to calm sheep at just 7 or 8 weeks old to see what they do. "Generally, they're interested and they watch the sheep, but they're so little they can't catch them. But if they're interested and want to engage in play, I want to encourage the pup that it's an okay thing."

Usually within a month or so, the dogs will indicate that they're ready to begin working, she says. "With Border collies, when they're puppies and playing, their tail is up in the air. They're not ready to be serious. When they're ready to settle down and work, the tail will come down."

When it's time to go to work, it's important to recognize each dog's individuality, Guthrie says. "You have to let it feel its way. What I've learned most about working with these dogs is that each is different. The biggest key is reading each dog and dealing with each individually—what it can handle, what can't it handle."

Most of her dogs have been successes. "They all have a strong work ethic; that's the genetic part," she says. Instinct is also crucial for livestock guardian dogs, which keep livestock—usually sheep and goats—safe from predators. They're not herders but they stay with the flock to fend off coyotes, wolves, dogs, and other dangers.

Most herding dogs have a strong work ethic thanks to genetics.

Above: *Stock dogs tend to be more gentle with sheep than with cattle. Dogs are allowed to nip, but not bite, at sheep.*

Right: *Stock dogs' instincts and ability might be considered amazing, but to the dogs, it's all in a day's work.*

Starting training while the dog is young is crucial, but an owner must take precautions, says Catherine de la Cruz, of the Great Pyrenees Club of America, which celebrates one of the most popular guardian dogs. "I don't advocate putting a puppy out alone with livestock. That's suicide. I put them in a pen where they're surrounded by sheep and then I put them on a leash two or three times a day to work with sheep," she says.

Livestock guardians do much more than predator control. "The value of a livestock dog is as much in letting you know something unusual is happening as in chasing away predators," de la Cruz says. "A sheep may get its horns caught in fencing or a heater may fall over and trap a lamb. A guardian will tell you, but it has to know the routine so it can tell you when something is not routine."

De la Cruz socializes her dogs with as many friendly people as possible. "They have to know what's normal in order to recognize what's abnormal. If they're not used to seeing people walk in to your place, you might have an accident on your hands. On the other hand, they may know that in the daytime people come in, but after it's night, it's not permitted. Then you have a dog who will use good common sense about how to protect."

In helping your dog to reach his full potential, it's important to know your dog and what he's able to do. "Working a dog should be pleasant for you and your dog," Bud Williams advises. "Know what your dog is capable of doing. Don't ask him to do things that he can't do. No matter how you try to hide it, he will know you are disappointed and both you and he will be unhappy."

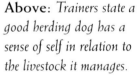

Above: *Trainers state a good herding dog has a sense of self in relation to the livestock it manages.*

Left: *"If you don't get a dog to stop what he's been bred to do for all those years and use that to help you, then you end up with a pretty good dog," says acclaimed trainer Bud Williams.*

Today's long-nosed rough-coated collies have more distinct features than the Farmcollies of yesterday.

Chapter 3
• •

FARMCOLLIES

RESCUE FROM EXTINCTION

Sheryl Chesney owes her life, or at least a limb or two, to a dog considered by many to be the ultimate farm dog, but is dangerously close to extinction. "When my brother and I were real small, about 6 and 8 years old, we were going fishing. We had to cross a cow pasture," says Chesney, of Glenn Springs, South Carolina. "We didn't realize we had to check if the bull was in the pasture, so we went walking across with our tackle and cane pole. Well, the bull charged us." Lad, her dog, fought the bull and kept it from harming the children. The dog suffered severe wounds but survived.

Lad was a Farmcollie, also known as the old farm shepherd, which was once the most popular dog in the country. These are the dogs that fiercely protect children, pluck tiny ducklings from dangerous water, and instinctively know what their people want without a word ever being said.

Farmcollies' natural instincts lead them to be protective of young livestock.

Farmcollies became a rarity as Americans moved from rural to urban areas and as farms and ranches began disappearing. The need for these all-purpose farm dogs all but ceased. "People no longer needed them for the purpose for which they had existed in the past," says J. Richard McDuffie, of Aiken, South Carolina, who has worked to revive the Farmcollie. "They no longer needed a general-purpose dog."

Instead, dog owners began preferring specialized companions—such as hunting dogs, guardian dogs, and herding dogs—but not a dog with all these traits rolled into one, according to the American Working Farmcollie Association, a group of Farmcollie admirers working to preserve the dogs.

A Farmcollie isn't a specific breed of dog, such as a Labrador retriever or Great Dane. "It's the instinct that's intact," Chesney explains of the dog whose nature is to herd, hunt, and guard. "That makes an all-around farm dog."

Farmcollie traits show up primarily in English and Australian shepherds, although other bloodlines may intermingle to make it possible to have a Farmcollie mutt. If that sounds a little confusing, it is. Chesney and other association members agree and explain it this way: Farmcollies are versatile descendants of the old Scotch collie and were indispensable to farmers during the nineteenth and early twentieth centuries. It was this dog that most Americans then thought of as a "collie," although they were very different physically from today's long-nosed Border collies.

The Farmcollie in this country most likely inherited the bloodlines of other types of herding and shepherd dogs that were brought by European immigrants, the

Above: *Rough collies are recognized by their long, pointed nose and full collar of fur.*

Left: *Intelligent puppies usually turn into intelligent, easily trainable farm dogs.*

association explains. But despite the intermingling, he retained his Scotch collie instincts and excelled in herding, guarding, predator control, and hunting.

"When I grew up in the 1930s and 1940s, they were everywhere," McDuffie says. "I began to realize in the 1970s that they were no longer prevalent." The Farmcollie was on the verge of extinction, though a few still remained.

McDuffie writes for *Full Cry* magazine, which is published monthly for hunting-dog enthusiasts, and began writing in the 1980s about extinct and nearly-extinct breeds, including Farmcollies. Readers sent him information about the dogs and he found a handful that still existed—one line in North Carolina and two in Tennessee.

"I located three families and acquired dogs from those three sources and started breeding," McDuffie says. "One family had had that strain of dog for 50 years."

He bought four pups—two males and two females—from that family and two females from

continued on page 42

The Farmcollie traits show up primarily in English and Australian shepherds.

Farm dogs come in all shapes, sizes, and abilities.

Farmcollies are companion, hunting, guardian, and herding dogs all rolled into one outstanding dog.

The Old English sheepdog is an adaptable, intelligent dog that never displays aggression, nervousness, or shyness.

Left: *The rough collie, the most familiar of collies, was popularized by the television show, Lassie, and played on the dogs' keen intelligence.*

Below: *Collies, who typically show a particular kinship toward children, are regarded by many as the ideal family companion.*

continued from page 38

The collie's popularity has placed him in the top half of American Kennel Club (AKC) registration rankings.

another family. His son, who also was interested in the dogs, acquired a male and two females. McDuffie developed Farmcollies with predominantly hunting instincts.

"We started breeding those three strains to develop dogs that would tree coons, 'possums, and squirrels," McDuffie says. "I was interested primarily in dogs that would hunt and tree game," McDuffie says. "I was not interested in herding dogs."

Chesney's family has maintained Farmcollies for more than 100 years. "The line just keeps going on for generations," she says. Lilly, one of her current dogs, is a descendent of Lad, the Farmcollie who protected her and her brother from that angry bull.

"Daddy says if a dog is good, it will herd what needs herding, chase off predators, and mother young stock—and that includes children," she says. "If they have all that, they're used in breeding."

A good Farmcollie is a valuable tool to a farmer, Chesney says. "They save a farmer so much time and effort. They also save stress on an animal because they don't run them to death," she says. "They don't chase or harass the livestock and what that equates to a farmer is profit. They're not running the pounds off your profit."

The Chesneys breed their dogs only when there's a demand, she says. "It's still hard to put all your pups in working farm homes, though you can come up with pet homes that will keep their instincts intact," she says.

A farm dog's instincts are in place from the time they're puppies and continue all their life.

A good Farmcollie will save stress on an animal because they don't chase or harass livestock. That means they don't run pounds off a farmer's profit, says Sheryl Chesney, a South Carolina Farmcollie advocate.

She's encouraged by stories of families who return to homesteading and seek to raise children in a more wholesome, rural environment around animals. "They need something to protect their livestock with, and some people are going back to Farmcollies," she says.

Farmcollies are perfect for that lifestyle because they're extraordinarily family-oriented, McDuffie says. "They're very attached to individual members of the family and they're very protective of children," he says. "When our son, who is now fifty-one, was ten or so, we had a female Farmcollie who stayed with him every where he went. If he moved two feet, she moved two feet. And if he and his buddies started wrestling, she would get hold of the other boy's pantleg and pull it."

Chesney had the same experience. "These dogs were our protectors when we were kids. We could not go fishing unless we took the dogs," she says. "They would kill snakes and keep other dogs away from us. Nothing touched us."

She also has stories of Farmcollies protecting children from snakes, keeping babies from tumbling down stairs, and gently carrying ducklings back to safety. "These dogs will protect you with their life," she says. "Whenever I hear stories like that, well, you just well up with pride because you know they're true."

Growing up and living on a farm is beneficial to keeping a collie's natural instincts intact.

Sheep dogs are not a particular breed, but rather a kind of dog, and can include kelpies, Australian shepherds, heelers, and more.

Chapter 4

SHEEP DOGS

"VERY MUCH AN EXTENSION OF YOU"

If you ask **Antonio and Molly Manzanares,** no two sheep dogs ever worked together better than Fats and Happy. These Border collie crosses began life together as littermates and continued a perfect partnership on the Manzanares' northern New Mexico sheep ranch.

"Fats was the male and Happy was the female and they worked in conjunction with each other even though they had different temperaments," Antonio says. "Fats was stubborn and overpowering and Happy had more finesse about the way she handled things. But when she had trouble with some sheep, he would come in and dominate the situation."

The dogs worked together to create an unbelievably good team, Antonio says. "That's when we were running more than one thousand head of sheep with just those dogs and one man controlling the whole flock. It was in pretty rough country, too, not open range. They would bring those sheep out of those areas and gather them and not leave anything behind."

Some sheep ranchers train their puppies by allowing them to take their cues from the older herding dogs.

Those dogs are long gone now, but their instinct and drive will never be forgotten. "Every other dog we have, we compare them to Fats and Happy. None ever comes close," Antonio says. It's no wonder that Fats and Happy were part Border collie. That breed has been developed for hundreds of years to gather sheep from rugged terrain with a practically unparalleled work ethic. Border collies

While innate livestock sense is bred into all good Australian shepherds, their working style varies.

Border collies are generally intelligent, alert, energetic, and responsive.

are tops among the sheep dogs; not the big, fuzzy breed, but among the dogs that herd sheep. Sheep dogs are not a particular breed, but rather a kind of dog that include kelpies, Australian shepherd, heelers, and more.

Herding dogs originated in Britain centuries ago and originally were large and powerful but difficult to control and rough with livestock. In the nineteenth century, shepherds and farmers wanted a more versatile, fleet-of-foot dog with a gentle disposition, strong nose, and keen eye. Several breeds were combined with this early herding stock; Whippet for good nose and speed and pointers and

Border collies have proven to be invaluable to stockmen.

Years of crossbreeding produced a dog with a gathering instinct and independence to work without constant direction.

setters for their strong eyes and nature.

All that crossbreeding eventually produced a dog with outstanding athletic ability, superior speed and movement, a gathering instinct, and the independence to work without constant direction. The first of what eventually would be known as the Border collie was revealed in 1894 by Adam Tefler on the English/Scottish border.

The Border collie's working style is distinctive as it moves with its head low to the ground,

The Border collie's working style is distinctive as it moves with its head low to the ground, its hindquarters high, and its tail tucked between its legs—all traits of its inherited breeding.

The Australian shepherd is valued by farmers and ranchers for its extraordinary instinct.

hindquarters high, and tail tucked between its legs—all traits of its inherited breeding. While innate livestock sense is bred into all good working collies, their working style varies, according to the American Border Collie Association. "They don't take their eyes off their sheep. Their intense gaze is focused on the stock, willing them to obey, to go where the dog directs them, to stop if the dog blocks their path," according to the association. "The stock [animals] aren't rushed or afraid, but they certainly respect the dog."

John Guynup, a longtime Oregon sheep producer, breeds and trains kelpie and border collie-cross dogs for herding both sheep and cattle. "Here we've found that the two basic breeds—Border collie and kelpie—are the best," he says. "When you work in sheep, the dog is very much an extension of you and every dog out there has to be reasonably well mannered."

Like the Manzanareses, his 2,800-acre ranch isn't open, flat country. "There's not a flat spot on the

Shetland sheepdogs are small, alert, and very intelligent herders.

Old English sheepdogs are excellent herders but are strong willed and need firm training.

Sheepdogs won't return home and rest until every one of their sheep are where they belong.

place. We have gullies, creeks, timber, and an elevation that averages six hundred to twelve hundred feet," he says. He relies on his sheep dogs to herd about 4,000 head of sheep to the correct pastures. "We run a lot of cattle, too, so we try to have dogs that run cattle, sheep, and goats," Guynup says.

Guynup's current favorite is a sheep dog he named Jerry. "He's just like a little terrier—all grit," he says. "He really tears into cows but he hasn't once bit into sheep. He's not the kind of finesse dog to bring in four or five sheep by himself, but put four thousand or five thousand in a pen and he's in his glory."

On the Manzanares sheep ranch, where they run about 850 head on national forest acreage, Border collies or Border collie crosses are their herding dogs of choice. "When the dogs are small, we look for a dog that has a good eye and some power to him to control what he's trying to herd," Antonio says.

Once the dog gets old enough to work, Antonio and Molly count on their instinct to get the job done.

Herding dogs originated in Britain centuries ago and originally were large and powerful but were difficult to control and rough with livestock.

"When the dogs are small, we look for a dog that has a good eye and some power to him to control what he's trying to herd," says sheep rancher Anthony Manzanares.

The Border collie can gather sheep from rugged terrain with a practically unparalleled work ethic.

Crossbreeding herding dogs eventually produced the Border collie, which has outstanding athletic ability, superior speed, and movement.

"We don't do a whole lot of training," Antonio says. "They hang out with us and take their cues from older dogs." Molly adds they have several herders working for them at various camps and they like to work the dogs their particular way.

Sometimes the dogs may use a little too much force and that's when corrective measures are required, Antonio says. "They can be aggressive. You have to discipline them. Some dogs have a tendency to want to bite. Normally, a Border collie will not want to hurt a sheep, but they might get a little more aggressive and nip at them. It's just a matter of discipline. They learn what's right. They're the smartest dog there is."

Nineteenth century shepherds and farmers wanted a more fleet-of-foot dog with a gentler disposition, strong nose, and keen eye. They combined several breeds with their herding stock—Whippet for good nose and speed, and pointers and setters for their strong eyes and nature.

"When you work in sheep, the dog is very much an extension of you and every dog out there has to be reasonably well mannered," says John Guynup, a sheep producer.

The working cow dog is unlike any other, say advocates of this aggressive canine with a work ethic that won't quit.

Chapter 5

COW DOGS

BRED FOR DETERMINATION AND A SHARP BITE

One of the most valuable, hardest-working members of a cattle ranch or farm requires no vacations, wage raises, or overtime pay. Just a pat on the head will suffice. Better yet, give him more work to do. Dogs on cattle farms and ranches easily earn their keep. Working cow dogs do the work of several men, save man hours, and move cows by causing the cattle the least amount of stress without running the weight off them.

Cow dogs are an invaluable tool and unique in that they typically have more nerve and bite than other dogs, says Oklahoma cowboy Ben Means, who has had cow dogs his entire life. "It takes a more determined dog to move cattle, especially if they don't want to be moved," Means says.

A cow dog isn't any particular breed. Rather, it's bred for working instinct rather than physical characteristics. Over the years, breeders

have produced different lines of working cow dogs from a variety of working stock dog breeds, such as Australian shepherd, Border collie, Catahoula, kelpie, and the Australian cattle dog to name a few.

Consequently, cow dogs may be a purebred or from a lineage of specialized crosses. This means they may be medium- or large-sized, shorthaired or long-haired, or light- or dark-colored. The things they do have in common are an unparalleled herding instinct, a drive to work, grit, determination, and a sharp bite to control cows that outweigh and outsize them many times over.

As a young man working his cattle ranch, Means realized that he needed a good, dependable dog to help him herd cattle. "A lot of times, it was just me and one horse, and that was not getting the job done. The area I lived in, people were not used to handling cattle," he says. Then he noticed a couple of cow dogs working some bulls. "I watched them and decided that's what I needed," Means says.

He approached the dogs' owner, Eldon King, and put his name on the list for a pup from the next litter. "That's where I got started with the King line of dogs because they're able to

Breeders have produced different lines of working cow dogs from a variety of working stock dog breeds, such as the Australian cattle dog, Australian shepherd, Border collie, Catahoula, and kelpie.

Cattle dogs have an unparalleled herding instinct, a drive to work, grit, determination, and a sharp bite to control cows that outweigh and outsize him many times over.

"That's really important that they're able to move whatever stock you're going to use them on," says cowboy Ben Means.

handle cattle," Means says. That dog, Ginger, began handling cows when she was about six months old and was fully trained within three or four months. "I trained her myself and we probably did things the hard way because I didn't know how. But I had trained bird dogs all through high school and always had coon hounds," Means recalls. "Even though I didn't know anything about it, we were

"Absolutely nothing will divert a good cow dog from his work," says Anna Guthrie, a stock dog trainer.

both pretty persistent. I had a good dog to start with. She learned in spite of me."

Cow dogs, especially those from a good line like Ginger, intuitively know what to do. "She had the instinct to go around and circle them and would bite to move cattle. That's really important that they're able to move whatever stock you're going to use them on," Means says. "They're the difference [that allows you] to handle cattle any time you want to handle cattle. Day or night."

As Means found out, a good cow dog more than makes up for help that you don't have. He can single-handedly control 75 head of cattle with one good cow dog and up to 250 with two dogs. "It definitely saves on manpower," he says. Over the years, his dogs—Susie, Buck, Kate, Queen, and Spot, to name a few—have successfully helped Means move his herds to where he wanted them.

Means has officially retired but still runs about 35 or 40 calves on his property and helps out on the ranch

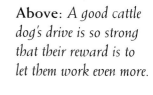
Above: *A good cattle dog's drive is so strong that their reward is to let them work even more.*

Left: *Cattle dogs are among the most valuable, hardest-working members of a cattle ranch or farm.*

Cow dogs may be a purebred or from a lineage of specialized crosses, which means that they may be medium-sized or large, short-haired or long-haired, or light-colored or dark.

Below: *A rancher can single-handedly control 75 head of cattle with one good cow dog and up to 250 cattle with two dogs.*

next door that runs about 5,000 cattle. He still relies on his dogs, especially one named Lena. "I use Lena when it's important to get it right and I don't want any mistakes," he says.

The working cow dog is unlike any other, say advocates of this aggressive canine with a work ethic that won't quit. Anna Guthrie, a stock dog trainer in Valley Center, California, discovered her dog, Riddle, was gravely ill only when the dog couldn't work.

Guthrie was en route to competition trials when she detoured to eastern Colorado to visit a friend. "We were just hanging out in the house watching TV when I saw cows where cows are not supposed to be," she recalls. About 30 of her friend's cows had gotten out of their pasture and were heading down the long driveway. The farthest cows were about 300 yards away and she sent Riddle and Riddle's niece, Trouble, to gather them.

"Riddle normally takes out like a rocket but that day she was moving slowly," Guthrie says. "She went about 30 yards and stopped and looked at me." Guthrie immediately knew something was very wrong and asked her friend where to find the nearest emergency veterinarian. It was about three hours away in Fort Collins, Colorado, at Colorado State University, which has a renowned veterinary school. Riddle underwent an ultrasound and emergency surgery at CSU where doctors discovered she had a ruptured uterine artery.

Not only were they able to save a very ill Riddle, but they also saved the nine puppies she was carrying. All were born healthy a few weeks later. The injury mystified Guthrie, who could only figure that Riddle must have caught her abdomen on the tailgate of her pickup truck and hit it hard enough to cause a rupture. "The only way I knew anything was wrong was because she didn't work," Guthrie says, adding that her dog is always ready to work. "If those cows hadn't gotten out, I would have never known."

Cow dogs are so driven that some will literally work themselves to death. Ben Means has had cow dogs of that caliber. "Usually the dogs, if they're the right kind, will put out everything they've got to the point of killing themselves," Means says. But that's not necessarily a good thing. "It puts a lot more responsibility on you to realize when the dog needs to be stopped and taken to water and rest."

An acquaintance of Guthrie's was taking his dog for water when he noticed that she was seriously injured. "He took her to the creek to let her stand in the water and he noticed blood coming out of her mouth," Guthrie says. That's a somewhat common occurrence because cow dogs frequently will bite their own tongue when they're biting at a cow. "But when he looked closer, he saw that she had been

Above: *A good cow dog more than makes up for help that you don't have, says cowboy Ben Means.*

Cow dogs are single-minded and take their herding responsibilities very seriously

Cattle ranchers must keep a close eye on their dogs because they're so driven that they literally will work themselves to death

kicked and had broken her jaw," Guthrie says. "She never stopped working and never gave any indication that she was hurt. Their drive is so strong and their reward is to let them work even more."

Absolutely nothing will divert a good cow dog from his work, Guthrie says. "You can have a female in full standing heat working right along an intact male and they'll keep working," she says. "He may, at most, steal a glance her way, but he won't stop working. They're just so driven."

Cattle dogs, especially those from a good breeding line, intuitively know what to do around livestock.

Cow dogs are good at working together to accomplish their duties.

Generations of breeding that characteristic into Border collies have produced some fine cow dogs, Guthrie says. "That's the genetic part. Over the years, I've come to appreciate genetics and what DNA can do," she says. "The next component on top of genetics is the handler or trainer and how they interact with that dog." Their personalities, style, and interaction can make the difference between a good cow dog and a great cow dog, she says. "It's just like people—some you click with more than others."

Cow dogs typically have more nerve and more bite than other dogs so they can move cattle that don't necessarily want to be moved.

Guardian livestock dogs typically stay with their livestock—usually sheep or goats—to deter predators.

Chapter 6

LIVESTOCK GUARDIAN DOG

KEEPING DANGER AT A DISTANCE

Catherine de la Cruz clearly recalls the day several years ago when she was calling Fancy, one of her dogs, to dinner. She called and called but the dog didn't appear, which was unusual behavior for Fancy, especially because it was dinnertime.

"I went out looking for her and it was a fairly remote place, so I walked a while," de la Cruz says. "Then I saw her. She came to the top of a hill, looked at me, turned around and walked away. I walked up there and found a feeder overturned with a lamb trapped under it."

A sheep apparently had tipped over the feeder and Fancy knew that the lamb needed help. "She stayed with it until I came," de la Cruz says. "She knew if she called me, I would come. When she just looked at me and turned around and walked away, that was her way of calling me."

The guardian dogs' job is keeping livestock safe by staying with the herd in isolated areas and aggressively warding off predators.

Livestock guardian dogs are not herders; their job is to protect the flock.

Rescuing that lamb was just another workday for Fancy, a Great Pyrenees, one of the livestock guarding breeds. The most common livestock guard dog (LGD) breeds are the Great Pyrenees, Akbash, and Komondor. Other LGD breeds are the Maremma and Anatolian shepherd.

Guardians typically stay with their livestock—usually sheep or goats—to deter predators. They also alert their farmer/rancher to dangers like Fancy did. Their duty is to the well-being of their flock, and LGDs are single-minded in their work.

LGDs are not herders. Herding dogs, aided by their handler, drive livestock from one area to another using aggressive tactics such as chasing, barking, and biting. The guardian dogs' job is to keep that livestock safe by staying with the herd in isolated areas and aggressively warding off predators. They're fiercely independent and generally don't need human help.

The Maremma is smaller compared to other LGD breeds but that doesn't mean they lack in their abilities to guard livestock.

De la Cruz's dog of choice is the Great Pyrenees, a large, white, majestic-looking breed that originated in the Pyrenees Mountains, which form the border between France and Spain. Pyrenees, also known as the Pyrenean Mountain Dog, were developed by Basques to safeguard their flocks from the wolves and bears that roamed the mountains.

The isolation of those European mountains developed the Pyrenees' independent nature, which proved beneficial to American farmers and ranchers hundreds of years later. With the tightening federal regulations in the 1970s on

Akbash dogs are very suspicious of strangers and will bark until their owners are alerted.

The Maremma's duty is the well-being of their flock. Like other livestock guardians, they are single-minded in their work.

predator control by poisoning, trapping, and aerial hunting, humans turned to the ancient method of using guardian dogs for livestock protection.

Great Pyrenees' territorial temperament usually means they feel responsible for livestock beyond their owners' property lines. Fancy, de la Cruz's Pyrenees, frequently visited a nearby dairy farm and would lie in the middle of the corralled cows. "One day, I heard a commotion in the dairy barn and Fancy went running over there," she says.

LGDs exude dominance over their livestock. Maremmas love protecting their flock and family.

As the dairy owner rushed toward the barn, he saw a coyote biting at panicked calves in individual pens, injuring ears, hindquarters, tails—anything he could sink his teeth into. Until Fancy arrived. "Fancy grabbed that coyote by the middle of the back and smashed him against the barn until he was dead," de la Cruz says. The grateful dairy owner credited Fancy with saving him thousands of dollars in livestock. To Fancy, she was just doing her job, no matter who owned the livestock.

The Komondor, one of the most unusual breeds in America, is a large, muscular, Hungarian dog covered with dense white

cords of long, curled fur. The fearless Komondor is a calm, alert dog who thrives on the responsibility of watching over something, whether it's livestock, cats, or a family. But if a threat arises, the Komondor becomes a bold protector and instantly springs into action, says Joy Levy, who was among the first to import Komondors into the United States in the 1950s. "They attack silently without a cry," she says.

The Maremma works very well with sheep.

Maremmas are very independent but loyal and protective over the entire farm.

Maremmas are known as being gentle, affectionate, and extraordinarily confident.

The Bernese mountain dog's ancestors were working farm dogs in Switzerland.

A Komondor's general appearance belies its guarding ability, Levy says. "To the average person visiting on the farm, they'll see them lying down a lot and they'll think they're slow with all that hair. But they spring into action in a way that you can't believe," she says. "They're constantly on guard whether they look like they're sleeping or not. They just don't exert themselves when it's not necessary."

Komondors sleep all day and work all night to patrol property and bark at anything that's not normal. "The farmer loves it because it means somebody is on duty," Levy says.

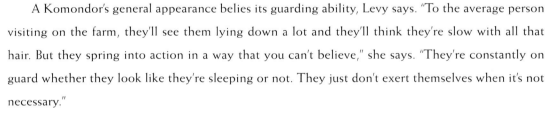

Komondors are also highly intelligent and can sense a threat even if no livestock is around. Levy knows this first hand. One night, Duna, their Komondor, was creating a terrible racket with incessant barking. Reprimanding him didn't help. When Levy's husband got up to see about the commotion, the dog pulled him by his pajamas to the front fence, just in time to see flames erupt from the top of the fieldhouse at the school across the street. Firefighters extinguished the flames and credited Duna with saving the fieldhouse. The Levys credit his persistence. "He had to tell us and we had to do something," she explains. Levy also attributes Duna's heroism to

his breed. "It was a cold foggy night and only Duna's sensitive nose and responsible behavior as an intelligent working dog resulted in such prompt control of a serious fire," she says.

Not all Komondor actions are so dramatic, but the well-being of others is dominant in their mind. For example, Komondors are not herding dogs, but if they're out with a large flock and they encounter a hazard, such as bad weather or fire, they'll gather the animals and lead them home, Levy says.

Despite its imposing size and fearlessness, the Komondor has a gentle side to its temperament, especially with animals who reside with it, Levy says. "They fall in love with the animals," she says. "If it's yours, it's theirs."

One farmer who raised miniature horses was afraid to let his Komondor get near the horses because he thought they were too delicate and could be easily injured by the large dog. His dog kept getting in with the horses, but he meant no harm: he would just lie among them, Levy says. The same farmer joined a mule society and was told that mules hated dogs, but his mule and Komondor were inseparable, she says. "They don't bug other animals," she says. "They like them."

This breed also befriends and charms feral farm cats and other less-than-cuddly animals. Levy lent a Komondor to one of her friends who had moved to the country with a neurotic cat that wanted nothing to do with the dog. "He couldn't stand that the cat didn't want to be with him," Levy says. "Well, within three days they were cuddling together and eating out of the same bowl."

The Akbash, which originated in Turkey, also is an ancient breed developed to fend off wolves and bears. This tall, athletic dog carries itself with a grace and elegance that belies its powerful personality. As with other LGDs, the Akbash is intelligent, independent, and capable of working without supervision, which appealed to Diane Spisak, an Akbash breeder who also raises sheep. "They've been bred for four thousand years to be independent of people," she says. "They can make decisions and react. They're not a 'step and fetch it' dog and they don't look to their owner for direction."

Spisak equates the Akbash with the Border collie in intelligence, although their jobs are much different. "With a Border collie, you can ask it to do something they know is wrong and they'll still work their heart out for you," she says. "If you ask the Akbash to do something stupid, they may do it once and then they'll look at you like you're an idiot."

The Akbash take their guardian duties seriously. A dog that Spisak sold to a Canadian sheep farmer faithfully brought the sheep home every night. One cold, snowy evening, the dog, Apollo, didn't come home with the flock so the farmer went looking for him. "He found the dog lying next to a dead lamb. He couldn't do anything to save her, but he protected her from the coyotes eating her," Spisak says. "Not until they picked up the sheep did he leave."

Both male and female Akbash are very motherly to baby animals, Spisak says. "In Colorado, an alpaca gave birth outside and it was raining. Alpacas don't like rain. She came into the shelter and abandoned her baby, but the dog stayed with the baby," Spisak says. "They're so maternal that they will stay with and protect livestock, especially babies."

One of Spisak's male dogs loves to announce the arrival of a new lamb, she says. "He's like a proud father. He'll always tell me when a new lamb is in the pasture by greeting me with a Lassie-like grin," she says. "He'll be like, 'Come with me,' and he takes me out to where the new lamb is. He's so full of himself when there's a new baby."

Above: *Guardian dogs, like this Belgian Malinois, always keep a keen eye on its surroundings.*

Left: *Bernese mountain dogs are recognized by its tri-coloring. It is black in color with russet markings over each eye, on the legs, cheeks, and on both sides of its white chest.*

Farm dogs work hard, and they play with much the same energy.

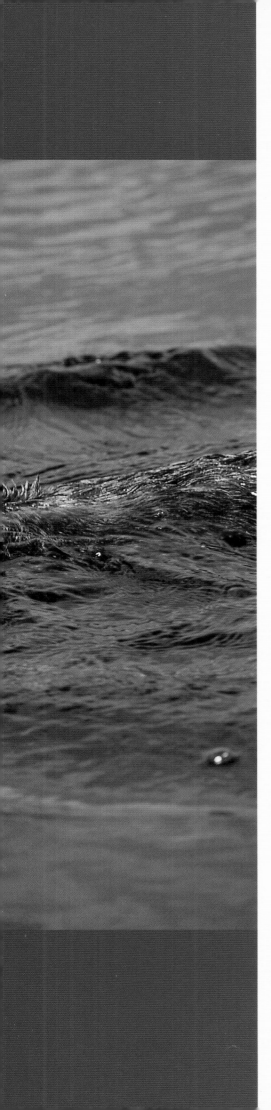

Chapter 7

ALL IN A DAY'S WORK

FOR FARM DOGS, THE EXTRAORDINARY IS ORDINARY

Acclaimed livestock handler Bud Williams of Texas said it best when he stated his stock dogs have done many remarkable things, but to them, they were simply doing their duty. With their keen instincts, high intelligence, and devotion to their families and handlers, farm dogs are capable of all kinds of extraordinary actions.

Some dogs, of course, are far more dramatic than others. It's exciting to read about a dog who saved his owner's life, but it's just as fulfilling to read of a cattle dog who put his life on the line for his livestock. Each act illustrates the farm dog's amazing capabilities.

"SHE SAVED ME'"

Sheryl Chesney's Farmcollie Lilly was just doing her job when she stood between Chesney and an angry sow. "Lilly saved me from a terrible pig bite," says Chesney, of North Carolina.

Lilly's protective nature kept Chesney from a painful ordeal. "A pig bite can be a terrible thing because they're rooting in dirt, which can cause all kinds of infection," she says. "They can cause deep puncture wounds. She saved me."

PROTECTING THE BABY

Chesney's family has had Farmcollies going back for generations because of their intelligence and devotion. "My mother's family had farm dogs and there's one in particular when she was little that she talks about still," Chesney says.

"There was one that kept her baby brother from going down a whole flight of stairs from the second floor. My grandmother would sit that baby on the landing and that dog would lie in front of the steps to keep him from falling," Chesney says. "My mother is in her eighties now and she still talks about that dog."

Many farm dogs have a natural affinity for the smallest members of the household.

ALLIGATOR BAIT

Chesney also recalls a story from some time back about a customer who bought a dog from her that ended up saving one of his other dogs—a Great Pyrenees puppy. After a long, hot day in the field, the Florida man stopped by a lake to let the dogs cool off and wade in the water.

The young Pyrenees didn't see the alligator rise out of the water, but Corey, the farm dog, did and jumped on top of the alligator to save the puppy. The gator grabbed Corey, rolled with him as gators do, and slid back under the water.

Right: *What could be better than growing up together on the farm?*

Below: *Farm dogs and children enjoy the benefits of having plenty of room to roam and explore.*

The distressed man knew he couldn't do anything to save Corey from the strong jaws of the alligator so he sadly picked up his puppy and got into his truck to head home. He was nearly home when he saw one of his hired hands who had caught up with him and asked, "Did you mean to leave your dog?" There with the employee was Corey, dazed and muddy from head to toe, but alive. The man was surprised, but Chesney isn't. "These dogs will protect you with their life," she says, "and he was protecting that pup."

FIREBUG

Chesney's last story dates back to when her husband was young. "This involved my husband's own dog," she says. Several decades ago someone was setting fires around their small community. Authorities figured that, as arsonists frequently do, he would sit back and watch the buildings burn.

84

Late one night, her husband's Farmcollie bulleted out to their yard and knocked down who she perceived as an intruder. Sure enough, the man had a can of gasoline and was coming into their yard. "He would have burned their barn, probably," Chesney says. "That dog knew. They know so much more than we give them credit for. You have to trust your dog."

When the work is done, it's nice to take a long, relaxing walk along a beautiful landscape.

TAKING CHARGE

Richard McDuffie of South Carolina and his son were riding horses one day, accompanied by an 11-month old farm dog. "He had run loose on the farm with horses all his life and had never had any occasion to heel one," McDuffie says.

When they returned to the trailer to go home, one horse inexplicably refused to load. Nothing McDuffie or his son did would make that horse load. Then the pup got involved. "He heeled that horse and put him right on the trailer," McDuffie says. "Couldn't believe it."

On another trail ride, one of McDuffie's friends approached a creek and her horse refused to cross. The farm dog, who also had never herded horses, heeled the animal and made him cross the creek. "You didn't have to teach these dogs to do certain things," McDuffie says. "They had the intelligence to figure out situations and do it on their own."

It doesn't matter what their people are doing, dogs always want to come along.

"WOULDN'T LEAVE HIS SHEEP"

Eunice Williams, who has worked stock alongside her husband, Bud, for more than 50 years, has seen her share of amazing stock dogs. This story, published in *The Ranch Dog Trainer*, illustrates how their herding dog, Buck, definitely took his job seriously.

"One day we were gathering a large pasture with about eight hundred ewes and lambs in it. This was country that included a lot of timber and logged over ground. We could see from a long way back that the sheep had taken the wrong fork in the trail so Bud sent Buck. By the time we got to the fork, the sheep were going the right way, but we couldn't see the dog. This wasn't too unusual since our dogs are expected to stay on the stock and not necessarily come back after turning them. When we got into the open country, we could see that Buck wasn't with them. We called several times, but finally

took the sheep on to the corral. We even went home to see if Buck was there. Bud finally went back to where he had last seen him and tracked him and about fifty sheep down into a rough canyon where there was a lot of down timber. Buck had them all under control, but he didn't know how to get them through the maze to bring them back to us. This was over two hours later [than the original drive]. He wouldn't have had any trouble hearing us call him, but he wouldn't leave his sheep. He was sure happy to see Bud, though."

This will no doubt be the start of a beautiful and long friendship.

WAITING FOR A MIRACLE

Ted Mandry of Washington, Missouri, was unloading debris about a quarter-mile from his house in 2004 when his parked tractor popped out of gear, rolled down a ravine, and toppled into a gully, trapping his right leg. He called and whistled for two hours, but nobody came.

His wife, Peggy, who assumed he was out mowing hay on their 80-acre farm, stepped out for a while and locked their dog, Shannon, a Border collie and golden retriever mix, in the house so she wouldn't chase the tractor.

Farm dogs may take a rest now and then, but they're always ready to jump up and get back to work.

Even as puppies farm dogs have instincts that will one day serve their families well.

When Peggy returned, Shannon was scratching and howling at the door, which was unusual behavior for her. As her cries became more persistent, Peggy put her on a leash to let her outdoors. When she opened the door, Shannon bolted outside and dragged Peggy through a pasture to the trees where Ted lay trapped and bleeding.

With their keen instincts and high intelligence, farm dogs are capable of all kinds of extraordinary actions.

Ted feared the worst would happen and that he would die before help could arrive. "I reached a point where there was either going to be a minor miracle or this was it for me," he told *Out Here* magazine. It was then that his wife and Shannon appeared at the edge of the gully.

Peggy called 911 and the emergency medical technicians spent about an hour freeing her husband. His leg had to be amputated above the knee, but his life was spared. He's still able to drive a tractor, though he no longer does heavy-duty work. Shannon was presented with the National Hero Dog award from the Society for the Prevention of Cruelty to Animals Los Angeles, which grants that honor to a heroic dog each year.

Farm dogs are devoted to their families and handlers, and the affection usually runs both ways.

"UP TO SOMETHING"

Vivian Flynt, a member of the English Shepherd Club, heard this story when she was editor of its newsletter, the *English Shepherd Advocate*. Cocoa, Dust-Dee, and Cyn-Dee, a trio of English Shepherds, knew these particular visitors to their farm were up to no good:

Theresa and David Kaschak of Pennsylvania are accustomed to visitors at their 100-acre dairy farm. Their English Shepherds are also used to farm agents, delivery drivers, puppy prospects, and any number of people popping in and out throughout the day at the Kaschak Farm.

When the pickup truck pulled in the driveway one morning, David and Theresa didn't give it much thought. What happened next certainly got their attention. As the man started to get out of the

Newfoundlands and spaniels, both water dogs, are also known for their sweetness.

The Newfoundland is as at home in water as it is on land.

truck, Cocoa ran up and leaped at his door. She smacked the door so hard he was knocked back into the cab. Barking like a maniac and showing her teeth, the normally mild-mannered Cocoa lunged at the open driver-side window. David held her back.

The man said he had been working on a township repaving project on a nearby road. As he gestured out the window, an enraged Cocoa tried to grab his arm. Their work was done, the man quickly explained, and they had a load of asphalt left over. He offered to pave the Kaschak's gravel drive for $1.75 a cubic foot. "It's a great deal," he told him. "You'd be fools not to take advantage of it."

But David was distracted by the pandemonium all around him. Not only was Cocoa going wild, their mahogany sable male Dust-Dee and their tricolor female Cyn-Dee were barking furiously and circling around and around the man's truck.

Their dogs' unusual reaction made the couple suspicious. Theresa excused herself, went inside the house, and quickly phoned the township. "No," the township secretary said, "there's no paving project going on in your area. We've heard there are scam artists working township residences, though." With Theresa on the line, the township secretary dialed the state police.

When Theresa glanced out the window, she was startled to see more trucks pulling into the driveway, including one pulling a pot of hot asphalt. There were a dozen men in all and they were pressuring David to let them asphalt the drive. He kept telling them "no."

But they were insistent. "Okay," the man said, "we're dumping our load of asphalt here and we expect to be paid." But none of the men would get out of their trucks. The English Shepherds made it plain that they would bite anyone who got out.

Finally, the men gave up and drove off. David gave them a bit of a head start and then took off after them in his pickup truck just to see which way they went.

That was all the information the state troopers needed and they took all the men into custody. The troopers explained that the asphalt was of extremely poor quality and would have hardened to a consistency of pudding, which would render their driveway unusable.

Theresa and David credit their English Shepherds, especially Cocoa, with watching out for them. "She knew that guy was up to something," Theresa said. "Having that many men come here was awful intimidating. I'm really glad the English Shepherds were around to protect us!"

Index